The Encyclopedia of Rock Chords

Wise Publications
London/New York/Paris/Sydney/Copenhagen/Madrid

Exclusive Distributo
Music Sales Limite
8/9 Frith Stre
London W1V 5TZ, Englan
Music Sales Pty Limite
120 Rothschild Avenu
Rosebery, NSW 2018, Australi
Music Sales Corporatio
257 Park Avenue South, New Yor
NY10010, United States of Americ

Order No. AM9259
ISBN 0-7119-4670
This book © Copyright 1997 by Wise Publicatior

Unauthorised reproduction of any part of this publication by ar
means including photocopying is an infringement of copyrigr

Cover design by Studio Twenty, Londc
Compiled and edited by Jack Lor
Music processed by Woodrow Editic

Printed in the United Kingdom I
Page Bros, Norwich, Norfo

Introductory Notes

1. The chords in this book are voiced in a way that makes them easy to find and play effectively. But that doesn't mean you can't play them differently if you want to.

    The notes contained in the right hand can be rearranged in any order you like, and will still represent the chord symbol shown, like this:

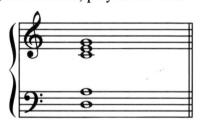

etc.

    The left hand can also be changed to alter the chord structure. Sometimes, when this is specifically required, the left hand alteration will be indicated by a 'cut' (or 'slash') chord, consisting of a chord symbol followed by a sloping line (the 'cut' or 'slash'), followed by the root, or bass note, that you need to play. C/E, for instance, means that a chord of C is to be played with an E root, or bass note.

    Here's one way of playing that:

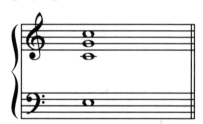

    In addition you will often see 'cut' chords containing a root not found in the chord itself. Am7/D, for instance, played like this:

is actually D11, described in a more commonly understood fashion for those who may not know what D11 means. Now, however, with the help of this book, you will never again have any trouble playing D11 – or, indeed, any other chords you're likely to be faced with!

2. All keys are covered here, except A♯. You will come across this key so rarely – if at all – that you only need to remember it's the same note as B♭, and any A♯ chords are played exactly the same way as their B♭ equivalents (e.g. A♯7 = B♭7, etc.).

3. ♭♭ is the sign for double flat, and means the note is to be lowered one tone.
    ✕ is the sign for double sharp, and means the note is to be raised one tone.

The C Collection

C major - C

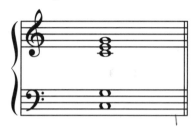
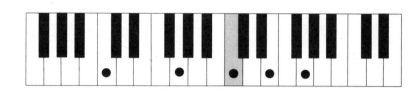

C suspended 4th - Csus or Csus4

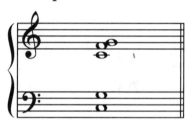
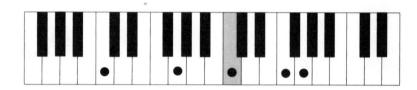

C augmented 5th - C+ or Caug

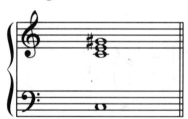
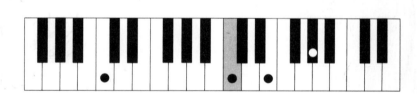

C added 6th - C6

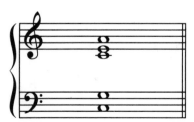
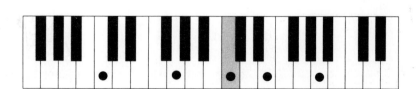

The C Collection

C major 7th - Cmaj7

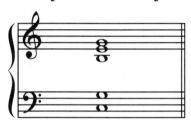

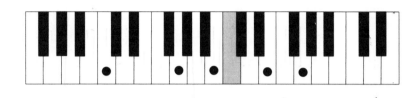

C dominant 7th - C7

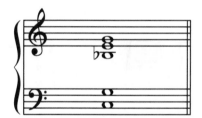

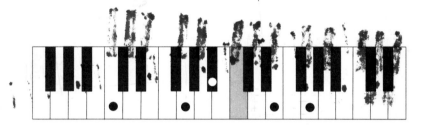

C dominant 7th with suspended 4th - C7sus or C7sus4

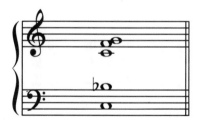

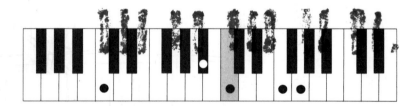

C dominant 7th with augmented 5th - C7+ or C7aug

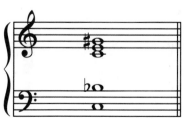

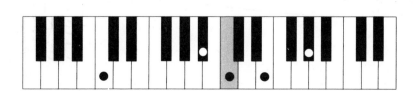

The C Collection

C dominant 7th with flattened 9th - C7(♭9)

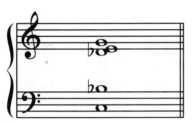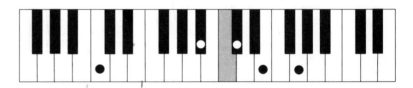

C added 9th - Cadd9

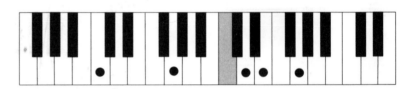

C major 9th - Cmaj9

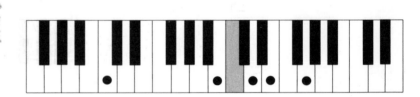

C dominant 9th - C9

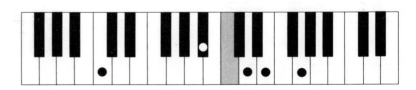

The C Collection

C dominant 9th with suspended 4th - C9sus or C9sus4

 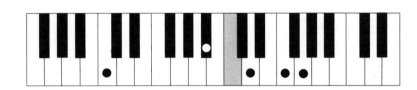

C dominant 9th with augmented 5th - C9+ or C9aug

 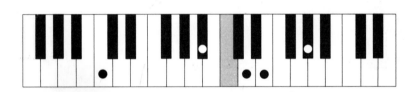

C dominant 11th - C11

C dominant 11th with flattened 9th - C11(♭9)

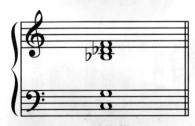 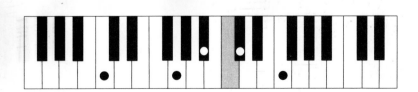

The C Collection

C dominant 13th - C13

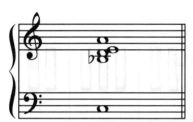

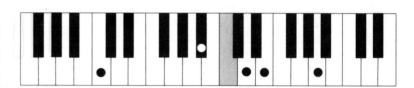

C minor - Cm

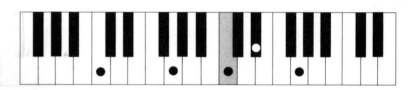

C diminished - C° or Cdim

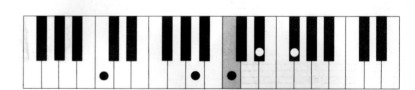

C minor added 6th - Cm6

The C Collection

C minor 7th - Cm7

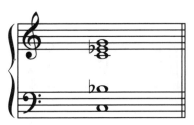 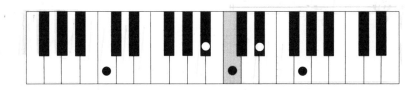

C minor 7th with flattened 5th - Cm7(♭5)

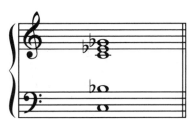 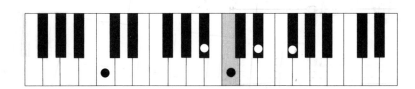

C minor added major 7th - Cm(maj7)

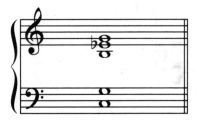 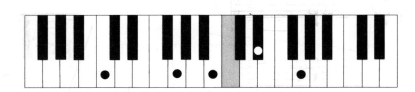

C minor 9th - Cm9

 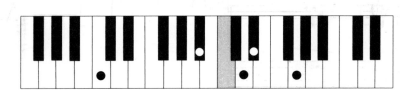

The C♯ Collection

C♯ major - C♯

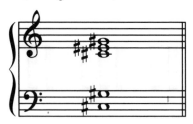

C♯ suspended 4th - C♯sus or C♯sus4

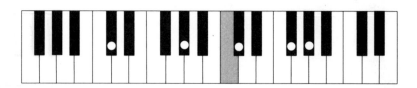

C♯ augmented 5th - C♯+ or C♯aug

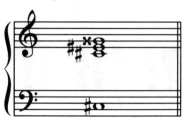

C♯ added 6th - C♯6

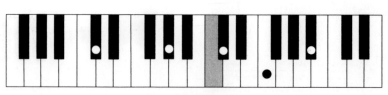

C♯ and D♭ are the same note spelled in different ways, depending on the key you are in.
For this reason, C♯ and D♭ chords are grouped together on facing pages.

The D♭ Collection

D♭ major - D♭

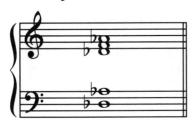

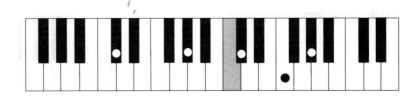

D♭ suspended 4th - D♭sus or D♭sus4

D♭ augmented 5th - D♭+ or D♭aug

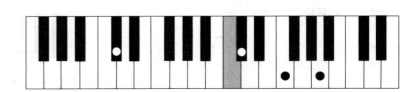

D♭ added 6th - D♭6

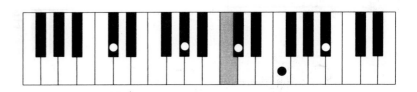

The C♯ Collection

C♯ major 7th - C♯maj7

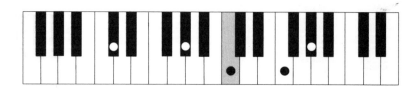

C♯ dominant 7th - C♯7

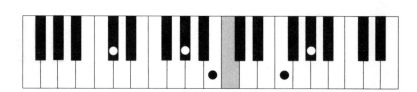

C♯ dominant 7th with suspended 4th - C♯7sus or C♯sus4

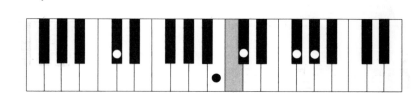

C♯ dominant 7th with augmented 5th - C♯7+ or C♯7aug

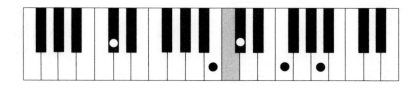

The D♭ Collection

D♭ major 7th - D♭maj7

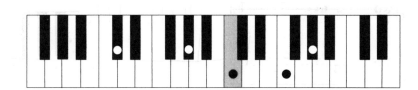

D♭ dominant 7th - D♭7

D♭ dominant 7th with suspended 4th - D♭7sus or D♭7sus4

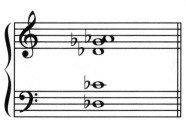

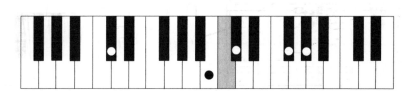

D♭ dominant 7th with augmented 5th - D♭7+ or D♭7aug

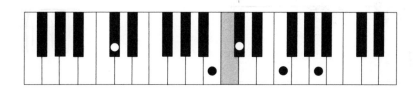

The C♯ Collection

C♯ dominant 7th with flattened 9th - C♯7(♭9)

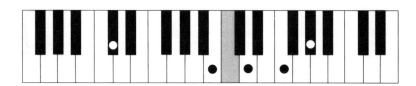

C♯ added 9th - C♯add9

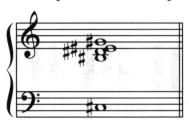

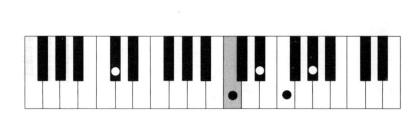

C♯ major 9th - C♯maj9

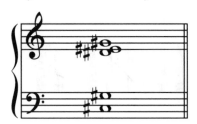

C♯ dominant 9th - C♯9

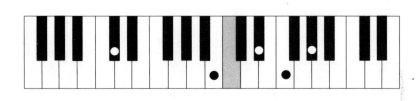

The D♭ Collection

D♭ dominant 7th with flattened 9th - D♭7(♭9)

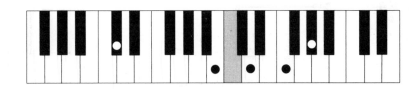

D♭ added 9th - D♭add9

D♭ major 9th - D♭maj9

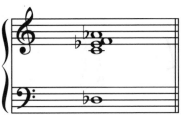
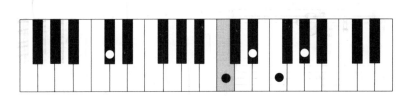

D♭ dominant 9th - D♭9

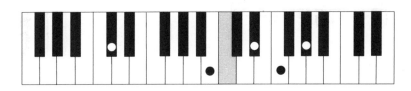

The C♯ Collection

C♯ dominant 9th with suspended 4th - C♯9sus or C♯9sus4

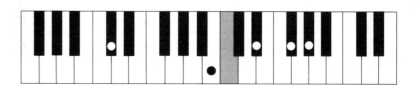

C♯ dominant 9th with augmented 5th - C♯9+ or C♯9aug

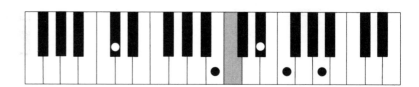

C♯ dominant 11th - C♯11

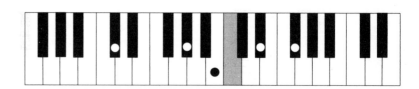

C♯ dominant 11th with flattened 9th - C♯11(♭9)

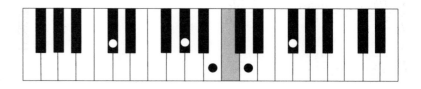

The D♭ Collection

Db dominant 9th with suspended 4th - Db9sus or Db9sus4

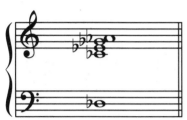

Db dominant 9th with augmented 5th - Db9+ or Db9aug

Db dominant 11th - Db11

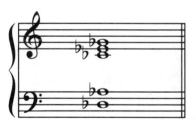
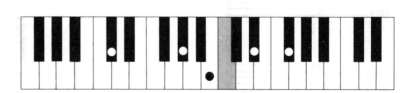

Db dominant 11th with flattened 9th - Db11(b9)

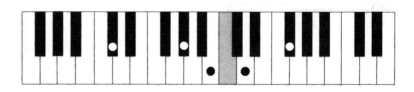

The C♯ Collection

C♯ dominant 13th - C♯13

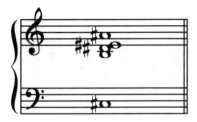

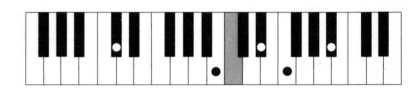

C♯ minor - C♯m

C♯ diminished - C♯° or C♯dim

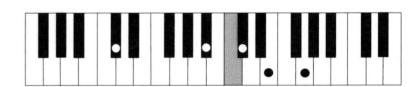

C♯ minor added 6th - C♯m6

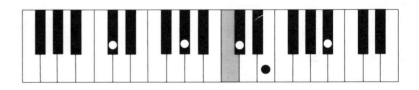

The D♭ Collection

D♭ dominant 13th - D♭13

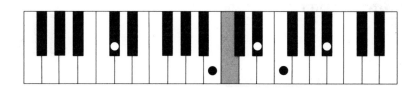

D♭ minor - D♭m

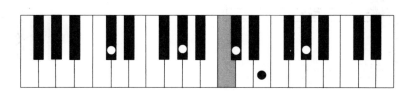

D♭ diminished - D♭° or D♭dim

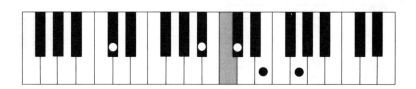

D♭ minor added 6th - D♭m6

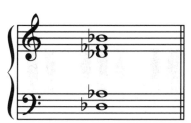

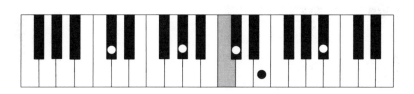

The C♯ Collection

C♯ minor 7th - C♯m7

C♯ minor 7th with flattened 5th - C♯m7(♭5)

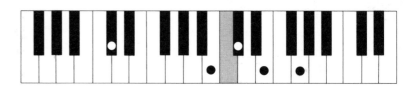

C♯ minor added major 7th - C♯m(maj7)

C♯ minor 9th - C♯m9

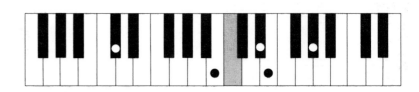

The D♭ Collection

D♭ minor 7th - D♭m7

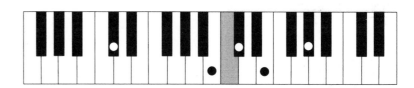

D♭ minor 7th with flattened 5th - D♭m7(♭5)

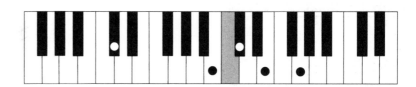

D♭ minor added major 7th - D♭m(maj7)

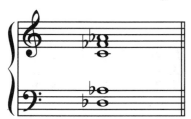

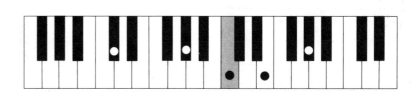

D♭ minor 9th - D♭m9

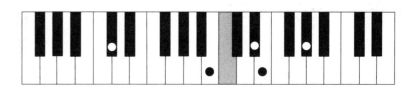

The D Collection

D major - D

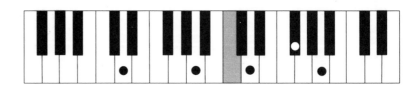

D suspended 4th - Dsus or Dsus4

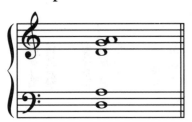

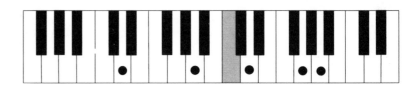

D augmented 5th - D+ or Daug

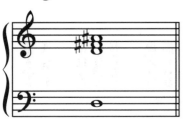

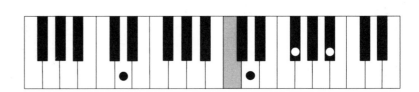

D added 6th - D6

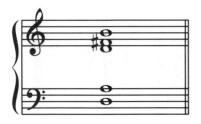

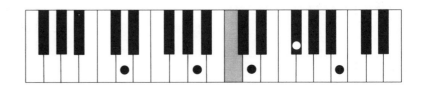

The D Collection

D major 7th - Dmaj7

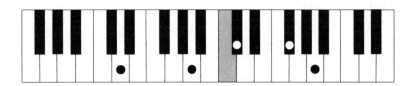

D dominant 7th - D7

D dominant 7th with suspended 4th - D7sus or D7sus4

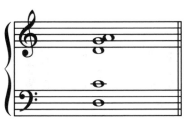

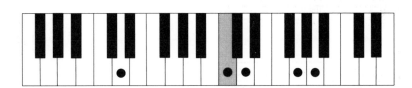

D dominant 7th with augmented 5th - D7+ or D7aug

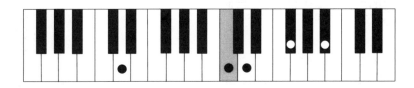

The D Collection

D dominant 7th with flattened 9th - D7(♭9)

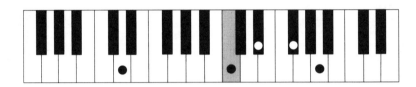

D added 9th - Dadd9

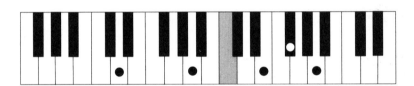

D major 9th - Dmaj9

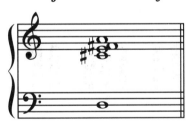

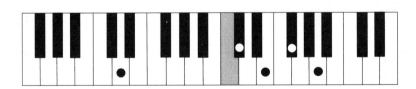

D dominant 9th - D9

The D Collection

D dominant 9th with suspended 4th - D9sus or D9sus4

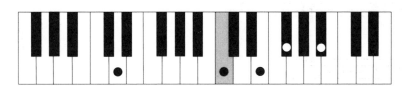

D dominant 9th with augmented 5th - D9+ or D9aug

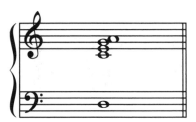

D dominant 11th - D11

D dominant 11th with flattened 9th - D11(♭9)

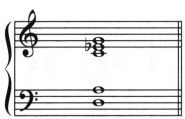

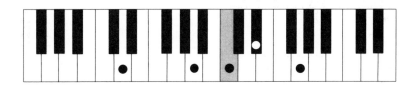

The D Collection

D dominant 13th - D13

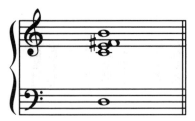

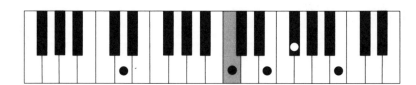

D minor - Dm

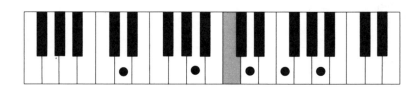

D diminished - D°or Ddim

D minor added 6th - Dm6

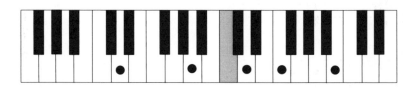

The D Collection

D minor 7th - Dm7

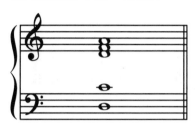
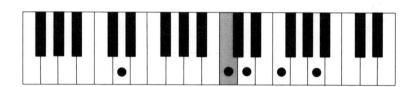

D minor 7th with flattened 5th - Dm7(♭5)

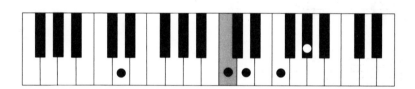

D minor added major 7th - Dm(maj7)

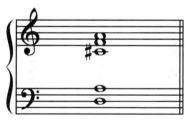
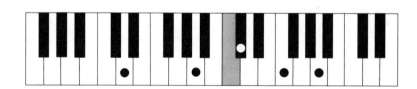

D minor 9th - Dm9

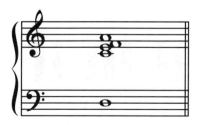
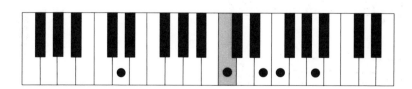

The D♯ Collection

D♯ major - D♯

D♯ suspended 4th - D♯sus or D♯sus4

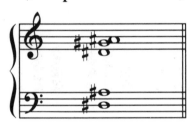

D♯ augmented 5th - D♯+ or D♯aug

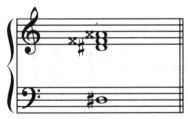

D♯ added 6th - D♯6

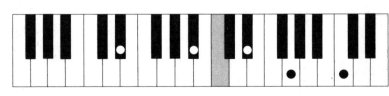

D♯ and E♭ are the same note spelled in different ways, depending on the key you are in.
For this reason, D♯ and E♭ chords are grouped together on facing pages.

The E♭ Collection

E♭ major - E♭

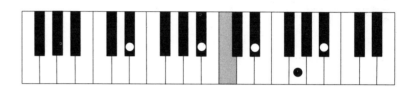

E♭ suspended 4th - E♭sus or E♭sus4

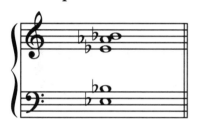

E♭ augmented 5th - E♭+ or E♭aug

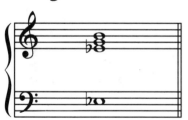

E♭ added 6th - E♭6

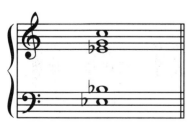

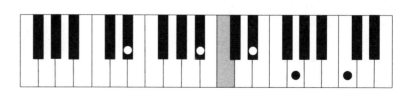

The D♯ Collection

D♯ major 7th - D♯maj7

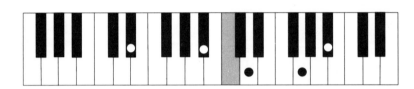

D♯ dominant 7th - D♯7

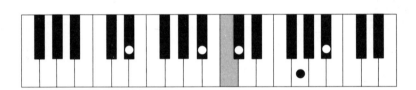

D♯ dominant 7th with suspended 4th - D♯7sus or D♯7sus4

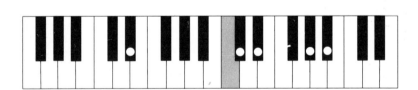

D♯ dominant 7th with augmented 5th - D♯7+ or D♯7aug

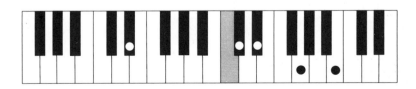

The E♭ Collection

E♭ major 7th - E♭maj7

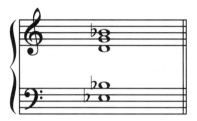

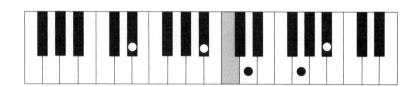

E♭ dominant 7th - E♭7

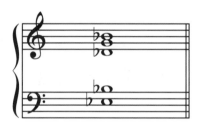

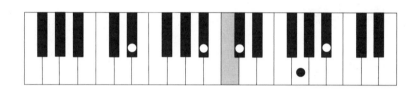

E♭ dominant 7th with suspended 4th - E♭7sus or E♭7sus4

E♭ dominant 7th with augmented 5th - E♭7+ or E♭7aug

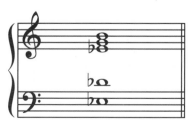

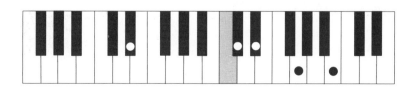

The D♯ Collection

D♯ dominant 7th with flattened 9th - D♯7(♭9)

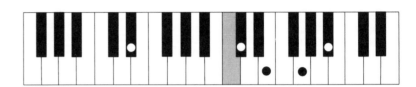

D♯ added 9th - D♯add9

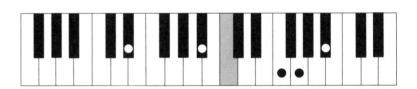

D♯ major 9th - D♯maj9

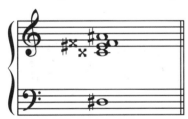

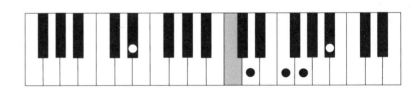

D♯ dominant 9th - D♯9

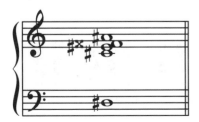

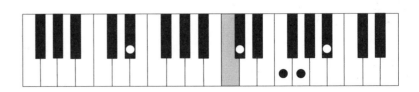

The E♭ Collection

E♭ dominant 7th with flattened 9th - E♭7(♭9)

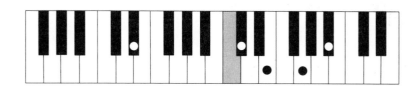

E♭ added 9th - E♭add9

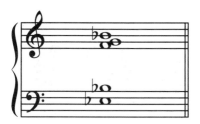

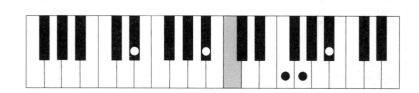

E♭ major 9th - E♭maj9

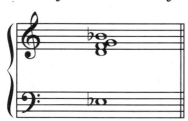

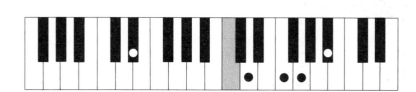

E♭ dominant 9th - E♭9

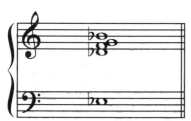

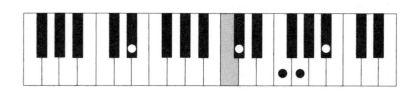

The D♯ Collection

D♯ dominant 9th with suspended 4th - D♯9sus or D♯9sus4

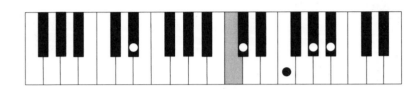

D♯ dominant 9th with augmented 5th - D♯9+ or D♯9aug

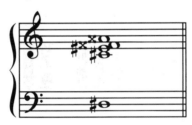

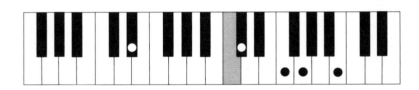

D♯ dominant 11th - D♯11

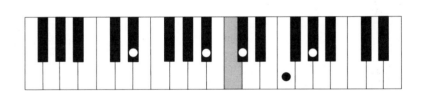

D♯ dominant 11th with flattened 9th - D♯11(♭9)

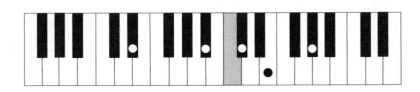

The E♭ Collection

E♭ dominant 9th with suspended 4th - E♭9sus or E♭9sus4

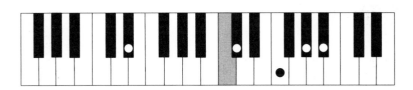

E♭ dominant 9th with augmented 5th - E♭9+ or E♭9aug

E♭ dominant 11th - E♭11

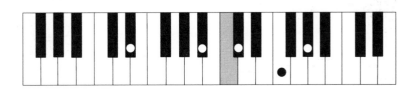

E♭ dominant 11th with flattened 9th - E♭11(♭9)

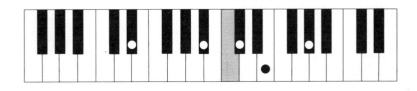

37

The D♯ Collection

D♯ dominant 13th - D♯13

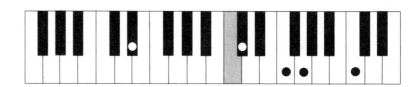

D♯ minor - D♯m

D♯ diminished - D♯° or D♯dim

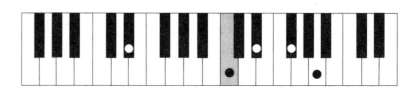

D♯ minor added 6th - D♯m6

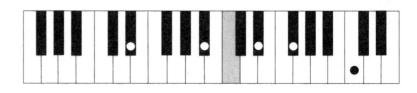

The E♭ Collection

E♭ dominant 13th - E♭13

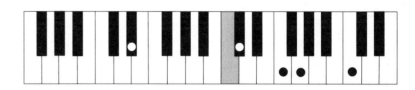

E♭ minor - E♭m

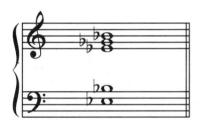
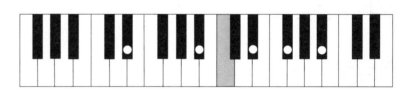

E♭ diminished - E♭° or E♭dim

E♭ minor added 6th - E♭m6

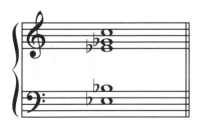

The D♯ Collection

D♯ minor 7th - D♯m7

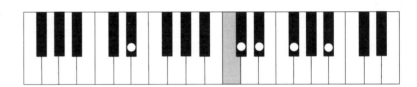

D♯ minor 7th with flattened 5th - D♯m7(♭5)

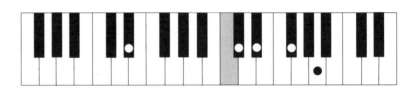

D♯ minor added major 7th - D♯m(maj7)

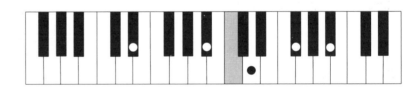

D♯ minor 9th - D♯m9

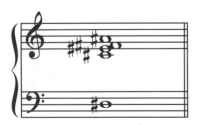
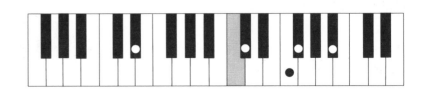

The E♭ Collection

E♭ minor 7th - E♭m7

 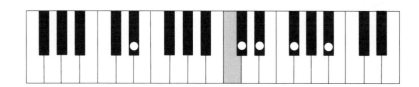

E♭ minor 7th with flattened 5th - E♭m7(♭5)

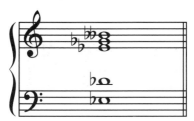 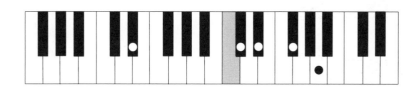

E♭ minor added major 7th - E♭m(maj7)

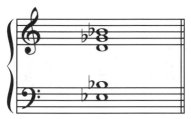 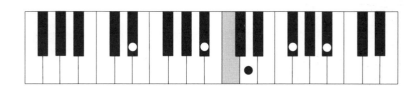

E♭ minor 9th - E♭m9

The E Collection

E major - E

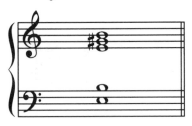

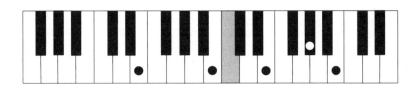

E suspended 4th - Esus or Esus4

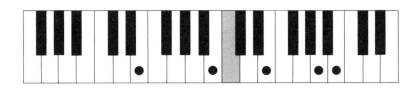

E augmented 5th - E+ or Eaug

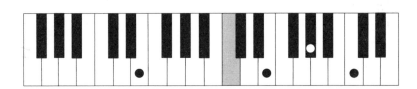

E added 6th - E6

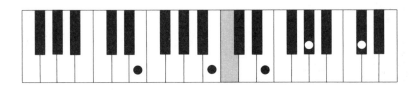

The E Collection

E major 7th - Emaj7

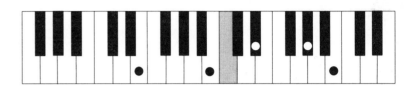

E dominant 7th - E7

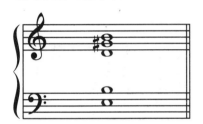

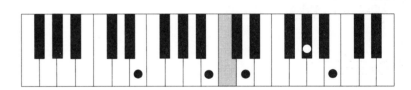

E dominant 7th with suspended 4th - E7sus or E7sus4

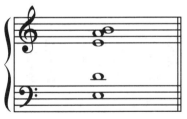

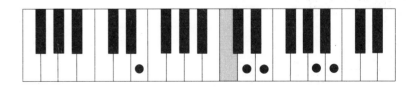

E dominant 7th with augmented 5th - E7+ or E7aug

The E Collection

E dominant 7th with flattened 9th - E7(♭9)

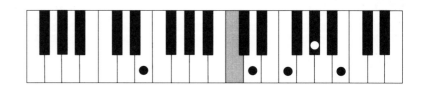

E added 9th - Eadd9

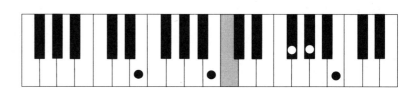

E major 9th - Emaj9

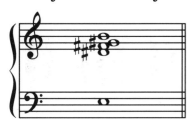

E dominant 9th - E9

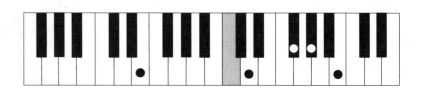

The E Collection

E dominant 9th with suspended 4th - E9sus or E9sus4

E dominant 9th with augmented 5th - E9+ or E9aug

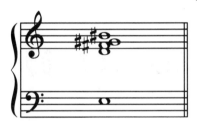

E dominant 11th - E11

E dominant 11th with flattened 9th - E11(♭9)

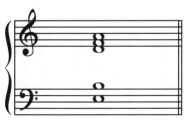

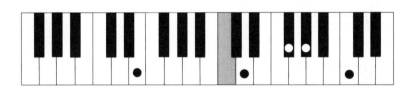

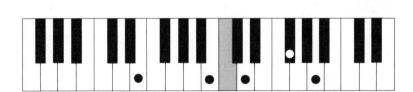

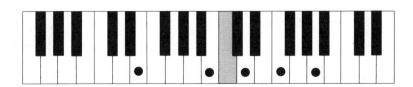

The E Collection

E dominant 13th - E13

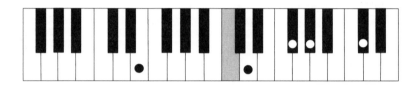

E minor - Em

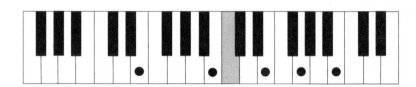

E diminished - E° or Edim

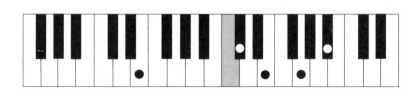

E minor added 6th - Em6

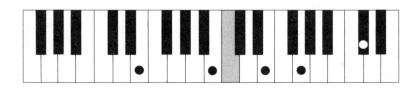

The E Collection

E minor 7th - Em7

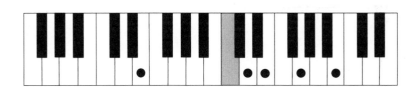

E minor 7th with flattened 5th - Em7(♭5)

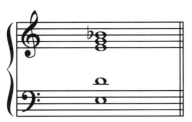
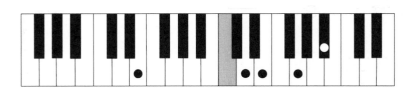

E minor added major 7th - Em(maj7)

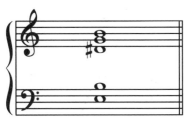
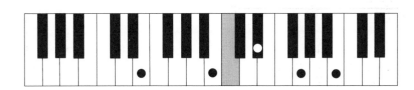

E minor 9th - Em9

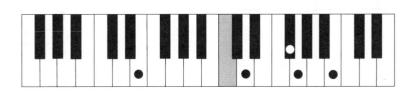

The F Collection

F major - F

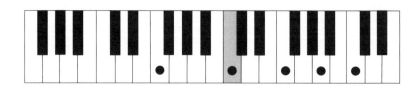

F suspended 4th - Fsus or Fsus4

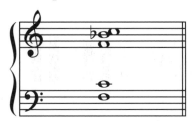

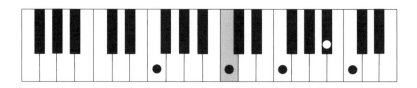

F augmented 5th - F+ or Faug

F added 6th - F6

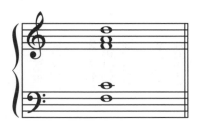

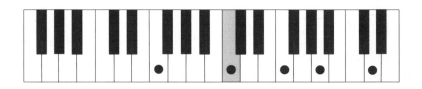

The F Collection

F major 7th - Fmaj7

 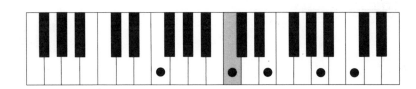

F dominant 7th - F7

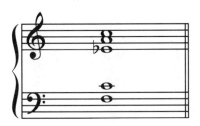 

F dominant 7th with suspended 4th - F7sus or F7sus4

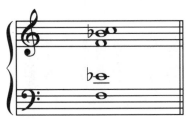 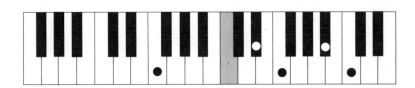

F dominant 7th with augmented 5th - F7+ or F7aug

 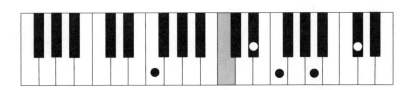

The F Collection

F dominant 7th with flattened 9th - F7(♭9)

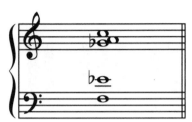

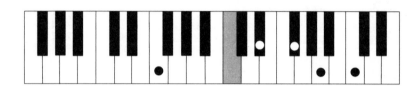

F added 9th - Fadd9

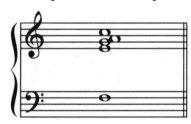

F major 9th - Fmaj9

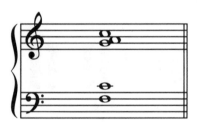

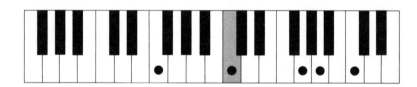

F dominant 9th - F9

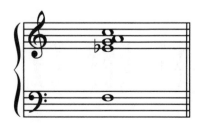

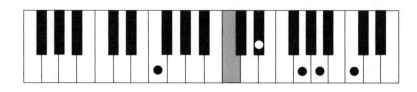

The F Collection

F dominant 9th with suspended 4th - F9sus or F9sus4

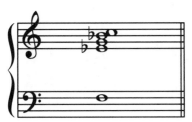

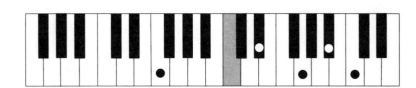

F dominant 9th with augmented 5th - F9+ or F9aug

F dominant 11th - F11

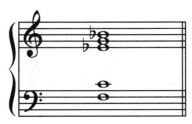

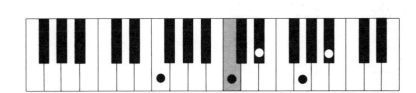

F dominant 11th with flattened 9th - F11(♭9)

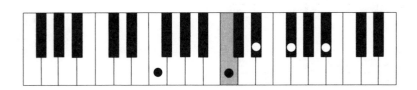

The F Collection

F dominant 13th - F13

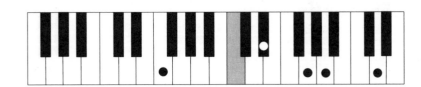

F minor - Fm

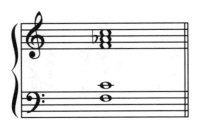

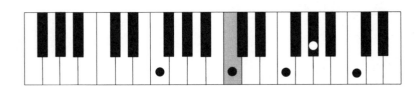

F diminished - F° or Fdim

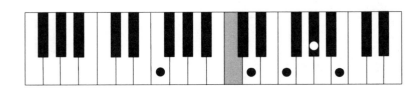

F minor added 6th - Fm6

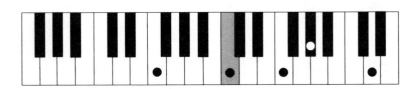

The F Collection

F minor 7th - Fm7

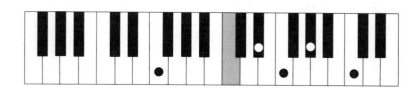

F minor 7th with flattened 5th - Fm7(♭5)

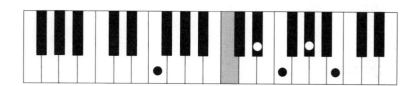

F minor added major 7th - Fm(maj7)

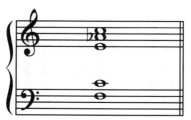

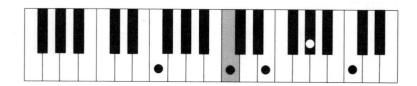

F minor 9th - Fm9

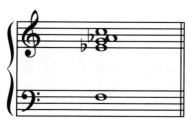

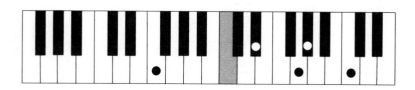

The F♯ Collection

F♯ major - F♯

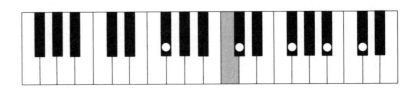

F♯ suspended 4th - F♯sus or F♯sus4

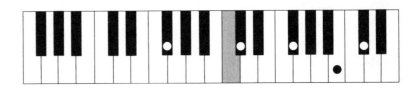

F♯ augmented 5th - F♯+ or F♯aug

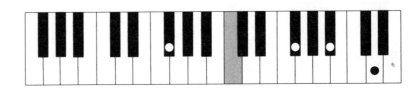

F♯ added 6th - F♯6

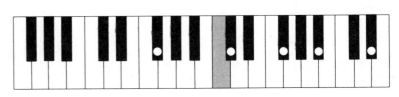

F♯ and G♭ are the same note spelled in different ways, depending on the key you are in.
For this reason, F♯ and G♭ chords are grouped together on facing pages.

The G♭ Collection

G♭ major - G♭

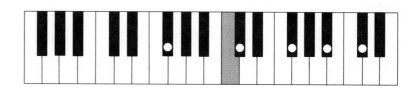

G♭ suspended 4th - G♭sus or G♭sus4

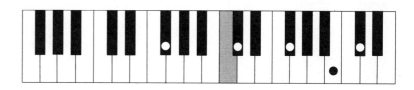

G♭ augmented 5th - G♭+ or G♭aug

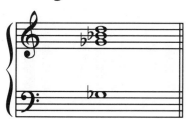

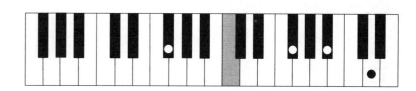

G♭ added 6th - G♭6

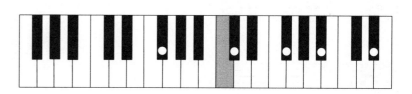

The F♯ Collection

F♯ major 7th - F♯maj7

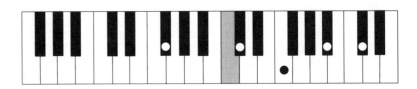

F♯ dominant 7th - F♯7

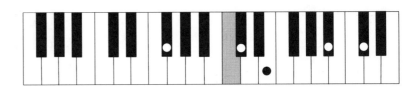

F♯ dominant 7th with suspended 4th - F♯7sus or F♯7sus4

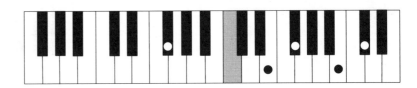

F♯ dominant 7th with augmented 5th - F♯7+ or F♯7aug

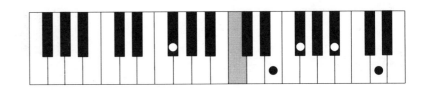

The G♭ Collection

G♭ major 7th - G♭maj7

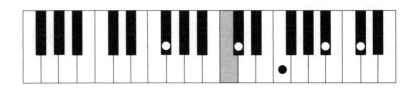

G♭ dominant 7th - G♭7

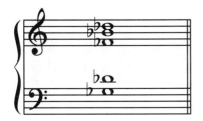

G♭ dominant 7th with suspended 4th - G♭7sus or G♭7sus4

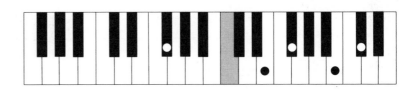

G♭ dominant 7th with augmented 5th - G♭7+ or G♭7aug

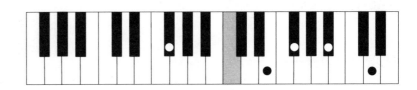

The F♯ Collection

F♯ dominant 7th with flattened 9th - F♯7(♭9)

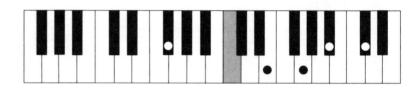

F♯ added 9th - F♯add9

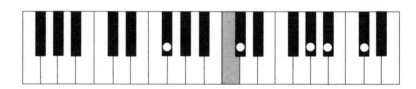

F♯ major 9th - F♯maj9

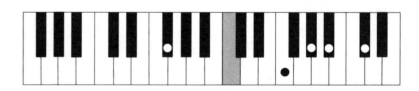

F♯ dominant 9th - F♯9

The G♭ Collection

G♭ dominant 7th with flattened 9th - G♭7(♭9)

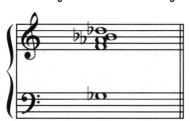

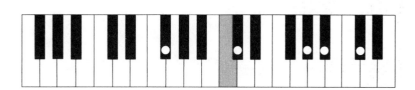

G♭ added 9th - G♭add9

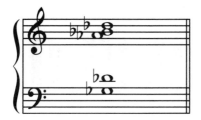

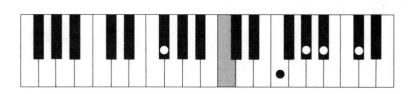

G♭ major 9th - G♭maj9

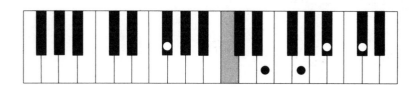

G♭ dominant 9th - G♭9

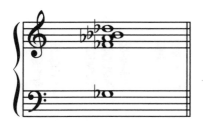

The F♯ Collection

F♯ dominant 9th with suspended 4th - F♯9sus or F♯9sus4

F♯ dominant 9th with augmented 5th - F♯9+ or F♯9aug

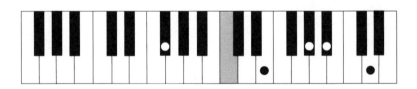

F♯ dominant 11th - F♯11

F♯ dominant 11th with flattened 9th - F♯11(♭9)

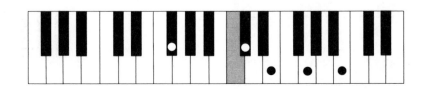

The G♭ Collection

Gb dominant 9th with suspended 4th - Gb9sus or Gb9sus4

Gb dominant 9th with augmented 5th - Gb9+ or Gb9aug

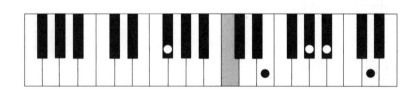

Gb dominant 11th - Gb11

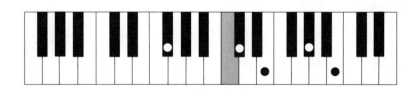

Gb dominant 11th with flattened 9th - Gb11(b9)

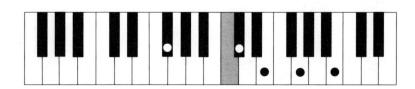

The F♯ Collection

F♯ dominant 13th - F♯13

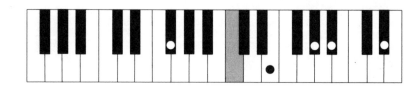

F♯ minor - F♯m

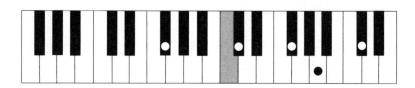

F♯ diminished - F♯° or F♯dim

F♯ minor added 6th - F♯m6

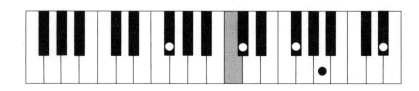

The G♭ Collection

Gb dominant 13th - Gb13

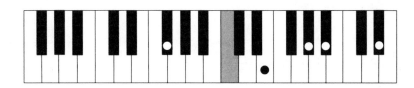

Gb minor - Gbm

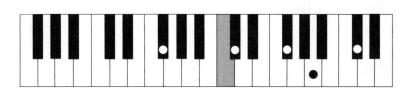

Gb diminished - Gb° or Gbdim

Gb minor added 6th - Gbm6

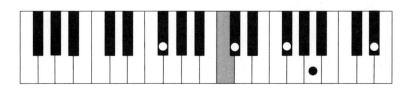

The F♯ Collection

F♯ minor 7th - F♯m7

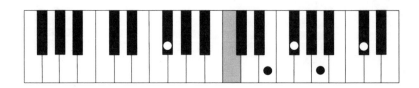

F♯ minor 7th with flattened 5th - F♯m7(♭5)

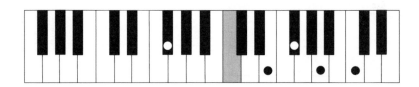

F♯ minor added major 7th - F♯m(maj7)

F♯ minor 9th - F♯m9

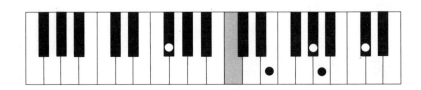

The G♭ Collection

G♭ minor 7th - G♭m7

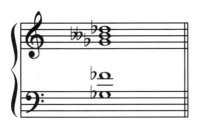
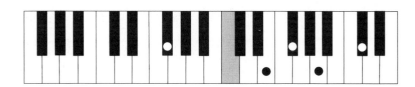

G♭ minor 7th with flattened 5th - G♭m7(♭5)

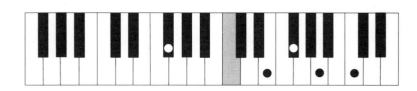

G♭ minor added major 7th - G♭m(maj7)

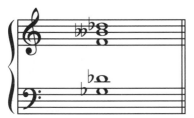

G♭ minor 9th - G♭m9

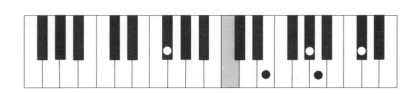

The G Collection

G major - G

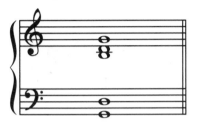

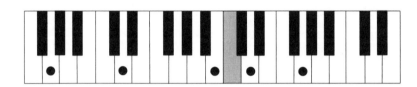

G suspended 4th - Gsus or Gsus4

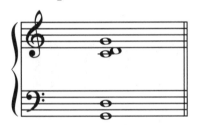

G augmented 5th - G+ or Gaug

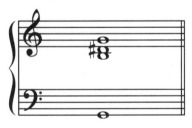

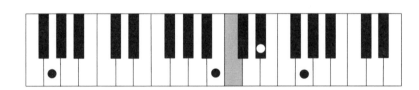

G added 6th - G6

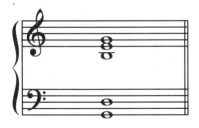

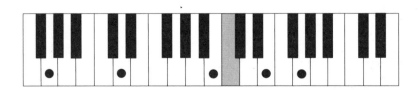

The G Collection

G major 7th - Gmaj7

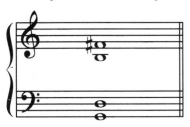

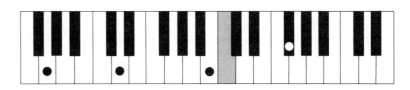

G dominant 7th - G7

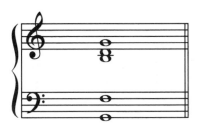

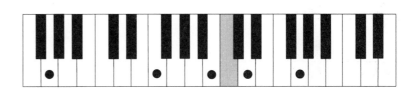

G dominant 7th with suspended 4th - G7sus or G7sus4

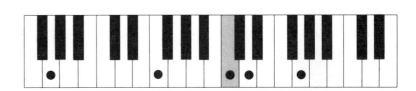

G dominant 7th with augmented 5th - G7+ or G7aug

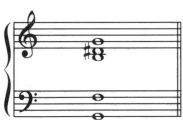

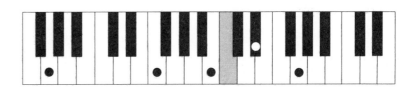

The G Collection

G dominant 7th with flattened 9th - G7(♭9)

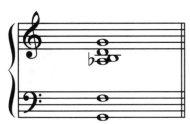

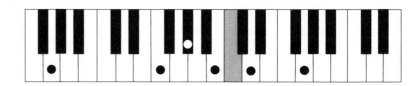

G added 9th - Gadd9

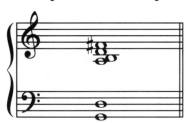

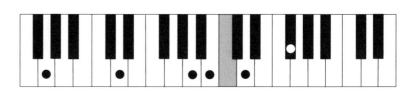

G major 9th - Gmaj9

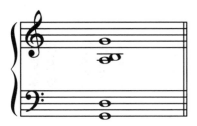

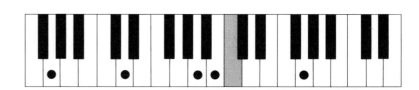

G dominant 9th - G9

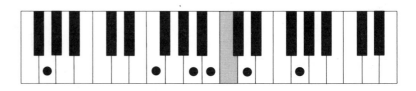

The G Collection

G dominant 9th with suspended 4th - G9sus or G9sus4

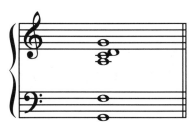
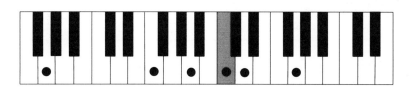

G dominant 9th with augmented 5th - G9+ or G9aug

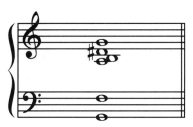
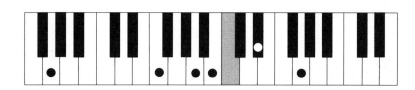

G dominant 11th - G11

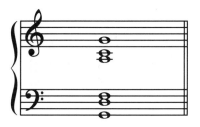
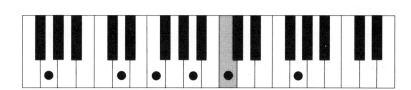

G dominant 11th with flattened 9th - G11(♭9)

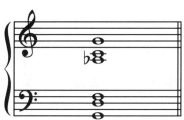
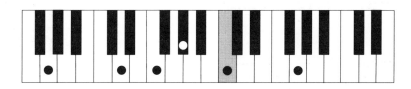

The G Collection

G dominant 13th - G13

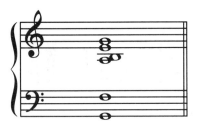

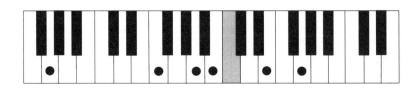

G minor - Gm

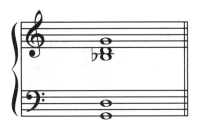

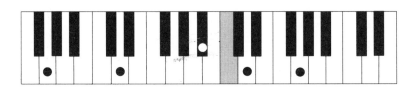

G diminished - G° or Gdim

G minor added 6th - Gm6

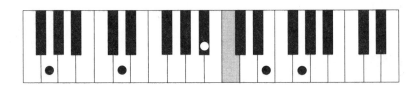

The G Collection

G minor 7th - Gm7

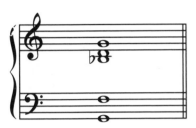

G minor 7th with flattened 5th - Gm7(♭5)

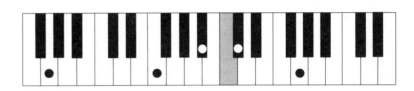

G minor added major 7th - Gm(maj7)

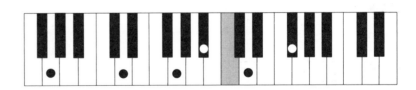

G minor 9th - Gm9

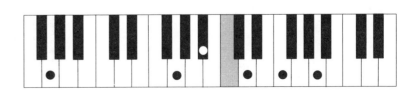

The G♯ Collection

G♯ major - G♯

 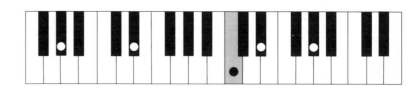

G♯ suspended 4th - G♯sus or G♯sus4

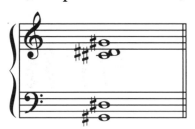 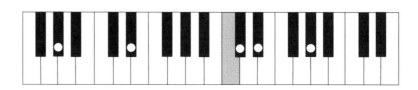

G♯ augmented 5th - G♯+ or G♯aug

 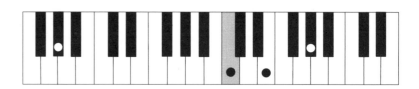

G♯ added 6th - G♯6

 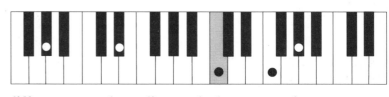

G♯ and A♭ are the same note spelled in different ways, depending on the key you are in.
For this reason, G♯ and A♭ chords are grouped together on facing pages.

The A♭ Collection

A♭ major - A♭

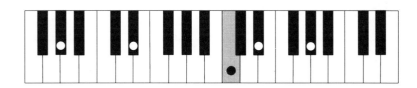

A♭ suspended 4th - A♭sus or A♭sus4

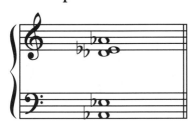

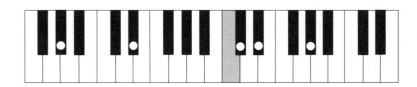

A♭ augmented 5th - A♭+ or A♭aug

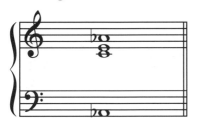

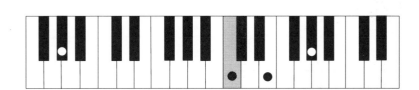

A♭ added 6th - A♭6

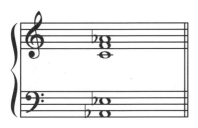

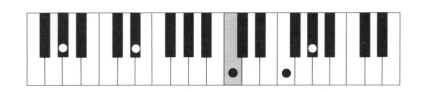

The G♯ Collection

G♯ major 7th - G♯maj7

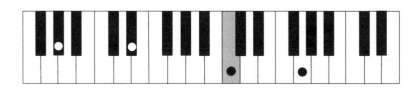

G♯ dominant 7th - G♯7

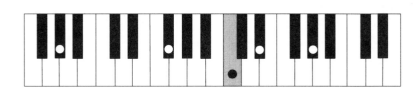

G♯ dominant 7th with suspended 4th - G♯7sus or G♯7sus4

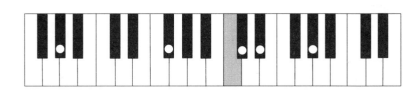

G♯ dominant 7th with augmented 5th - G♯7+ or G♯7aug

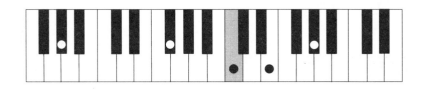

The A♭ Collection

A♭ major 7th - A♭maj7

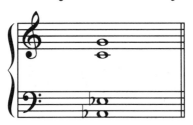

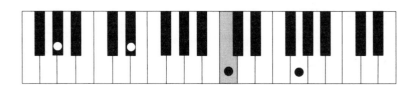

A♭ dominant 7th - A♭7

A♭ dominant 7th with suspended 4th - A♭7sus or A♭7sus4

A♭ dominant 7th with augmented 5th - A♭7+ or A♭7aug

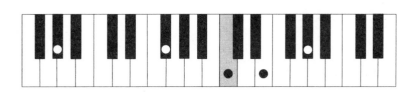

The G♯ Collection

G♯ dominant 7th with flattened 9th - G♯7(♭9)

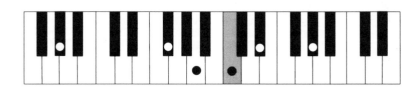

G♯ added 9th - G♯add9

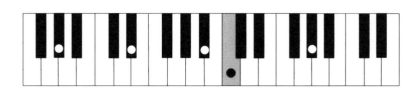

G♯ major 9th - G♯maj9

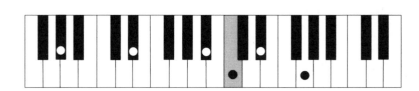

G♯ dominant 9th - G♯9

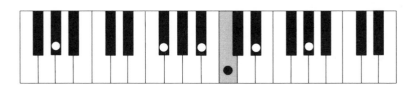

The A♭ Collection

A♭ dominant 7th with flattened 9th - A♭7(♭9)

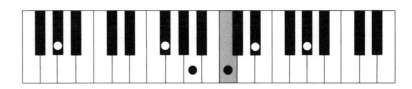

A♭ added 9th - A♭add9

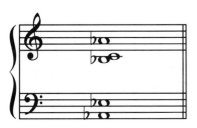

A♭ major 9th - A♭maj9

A♭ dominant 9th - A♭9

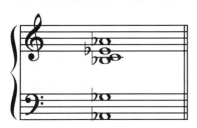

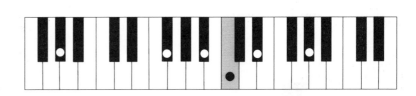

The G♯ Collection

G♯ dominant 9th with suspended 4th - G♯9sus or G♯9sus4

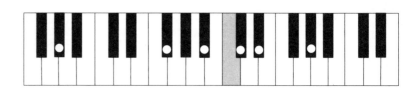

G♯ dominant 9th with augmented 5th - G♯9+ or G♯9aug

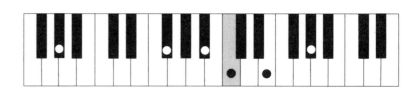

G♯ dominant 11th - G♯11

G♯ dominant 11th with flattened 9th - G♯11(♭9)

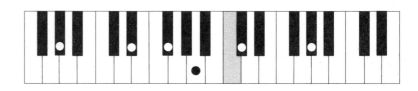

The A♭ Collection

A♭ dominant 9th with suspended 4th - A♭9sus or A♭9sus4

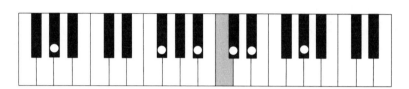

A♭ dominant 9th with augmented 5th - A♭9+ or A♭9aug

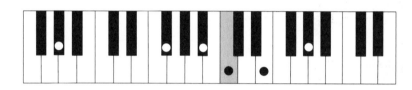

A♭ dominant 11th - A♭11

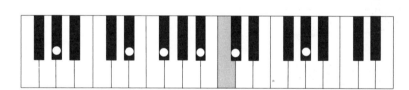

A♭ dominant 11th with flattened 9th - A♭11(♭9)

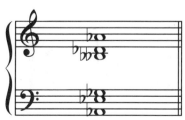
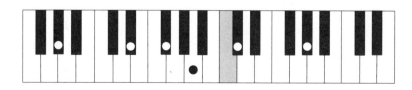

The G♯ Collection

G♯ dominant 13th - G♯13

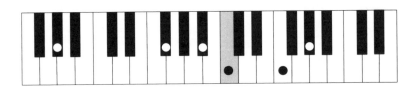

G♯ minor - G♯m

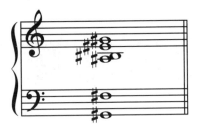

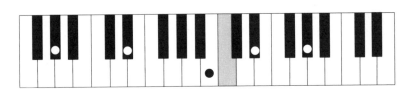

G♯ diminished - G♯° or G♯dim

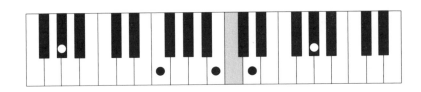

G♯ minor added 6th - G♯m6

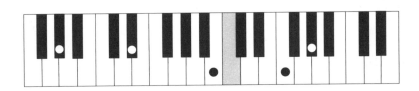

The A♭ Collection

A♭ dominant 13th - A♭13

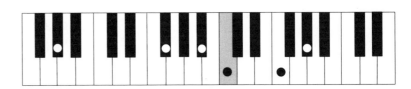

A♭ minor - A♭m

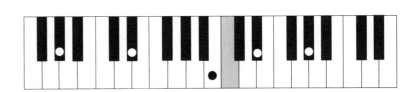

A♭ diminished - A♭° or A♭dim

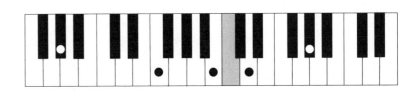

A♭ minor added 6th - A♭m6

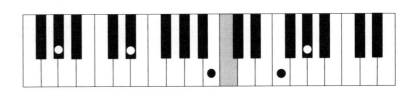

G♯ minor 7th - G♯m7

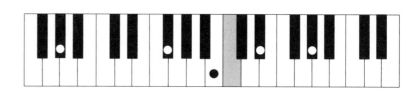

G♯ minor 7th with flattened 5th - G♯m7(♭5)

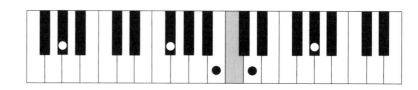

G♯ minor added major 7th - G♯m(maj7)

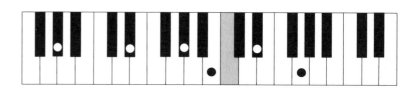

G♯ minor 9th - G♯m9

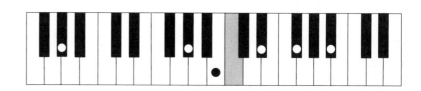

The A♭ Collection

A♭ minor 7th - A♭m7

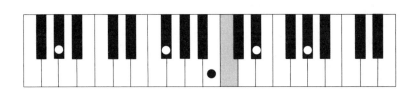

A♭ minor 7th with flattened 5th - A♭m7(♭5)

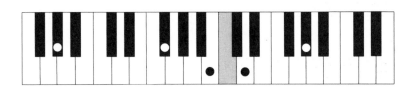

A♭ minor added major 7th - A♭m(maj7)

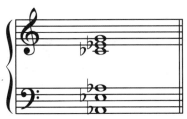
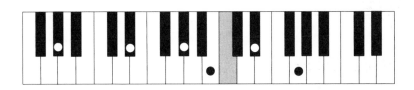

A♭ minor 9th - A♭m9

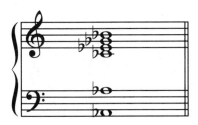
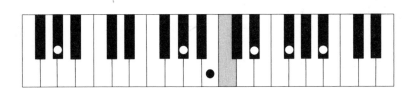

The A Collection

A major - A

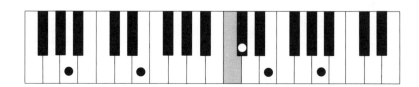

A suspended 4th - Asus or Asus4

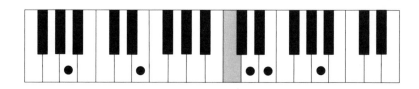

A augmented 5th - A+ or Aaug

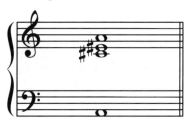

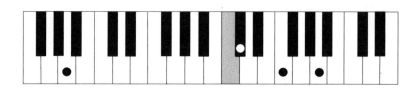

A added 6th - A6

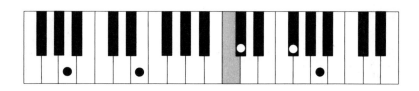

The A Collection

A major 7th - Amaj7

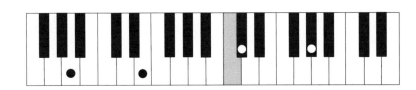

A dominant 7th - A7

A dominant 7th with suspended 4th - A7sus or A7sus4

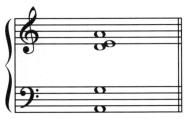

A dominant 7th with augmented 5th - A7+ or A7aug

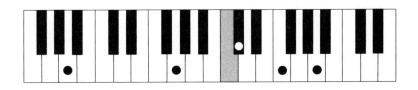

The A Collection

A dominant 7th with flattened 9th - A7(♭9)

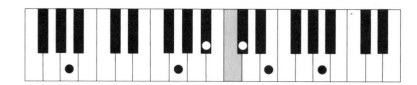

A added 9th - Aadd9

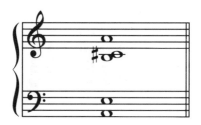

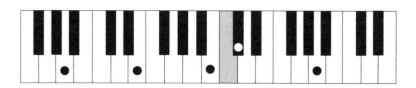

A major 9th - Amaj9

A dominant 9th - A9

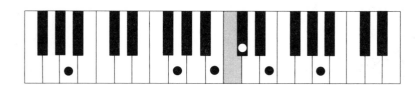

The A Collection

A dominant 9th with suspended 4th - A9sus or A9sus4

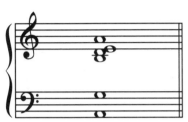

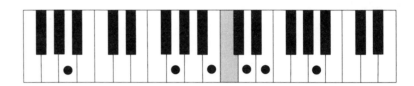

A dominant 9th with augmented 5th - A9+ or A9aug

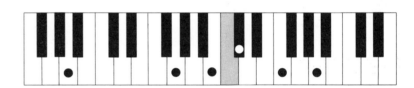

A dominant 11th - A11

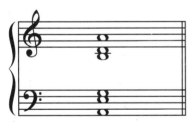

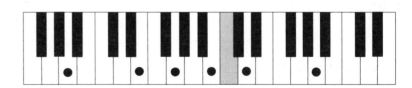

A dominant 11th with flattened 9th - A11(♭9)

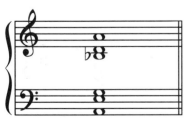

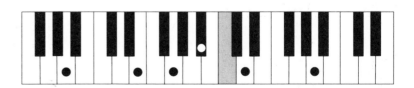

The A Collection

A dominant 13th - A13

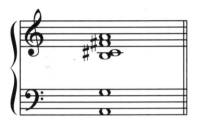
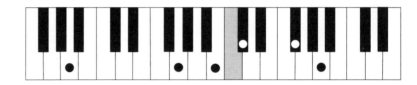

A minor - Am

A diminished - A° or Adim

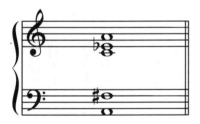
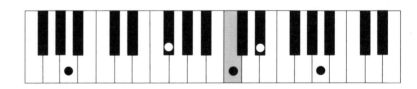

A minor added 6th - Am6

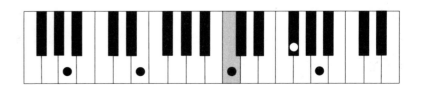

The A Collection

A minor 7th - Am7

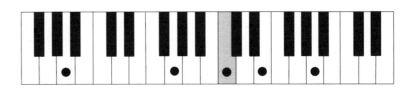

A minor 7th with flattened 5th - Am7(♭5)

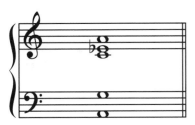

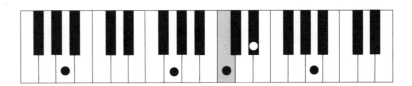

A minor added major 7th - Am(maj7)

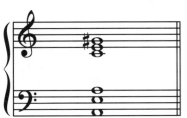

A minor 9th - Am9

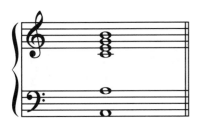

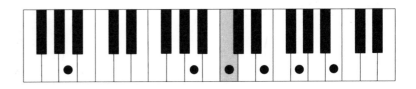

The B♭ Collection

Bb major - Bb

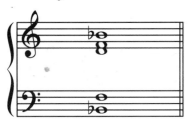

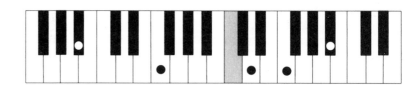

Bb suspended 4th - Bbsus or Bbsus4

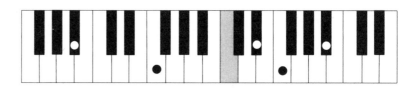

Bb augmented 5th - Bb+ or Bbaug

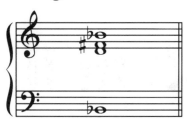

Bb added 6th - Bb6

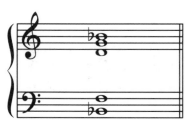

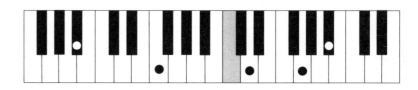

The B♭ Collection

B♭ major 7th - B♭maj7

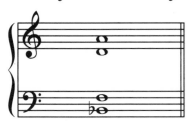

B♭ dominant 7th - B♭7

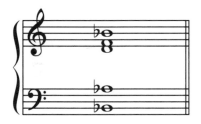

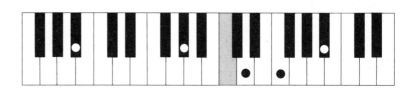

B♭ dominant 7th with suspended 4th - B♭7sus or B♭7sus4

B♭ dominant 7th with augmented 5th - B♭7+ or B♭7aug

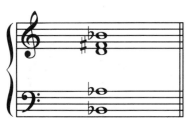

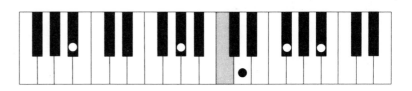

The B♭ Collection

B♭ dominant 7th with flattened 9th - B♭7(♭9)

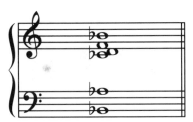

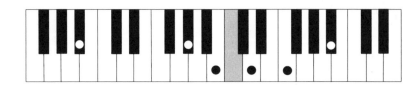

B♭ added 9th - B♭add9

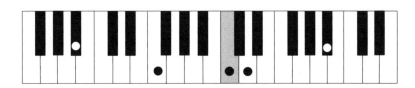

B♭ major 9th - B♭maj9

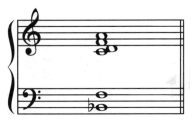

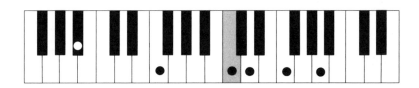

B♭ dominant 9th - B♭9

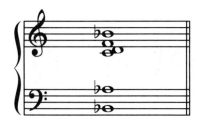

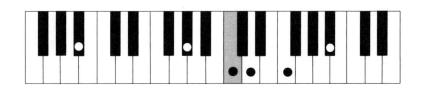

The B♭ Collection

B♭ dominant 9th with suspended 4th - B♭9sus B♭9sus4

B♭ dominant 9th with augmented 5th - B♭9+ or B♭9aug

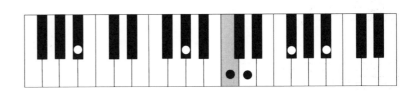

B♭ dominant 11th - B♭11

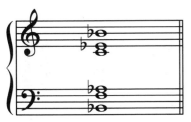
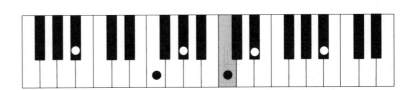

B♭ dominant 11th with flattened 9th - B♭11(♭9)

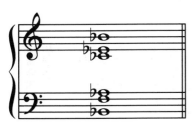
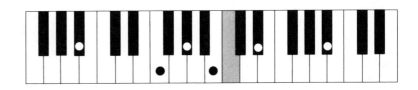

The B♭ Collection

B♭ dominant 13th - B♭13

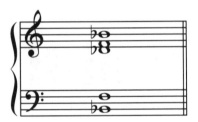

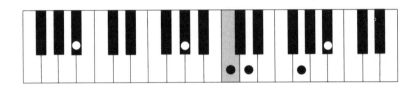

B♭ minor - B♭m

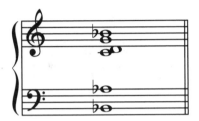

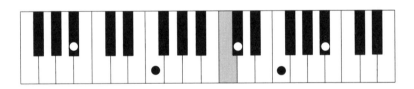

B♭ diminished - B♭° or B♭dim

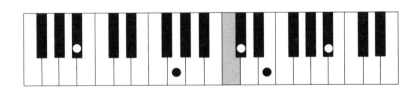

B♭ minor added 6th - B♭m6

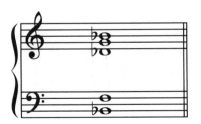

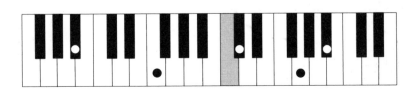

The B♭ Collection

B♭ minor 7th - B♭m7

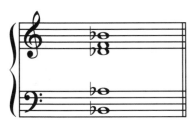
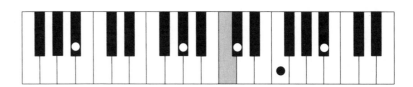

B♭ minor 7th with flattened 5th - B♭m7(♭5)

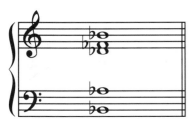
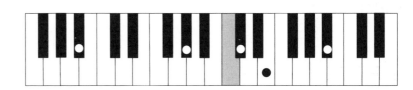

B♭ minor added major 7th - B♭m(maj7)

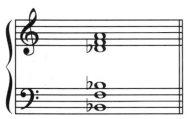
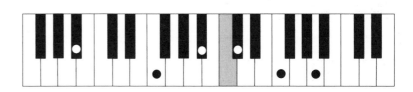

B♭ minor 9th - B♭m9

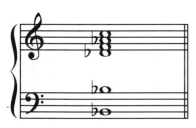
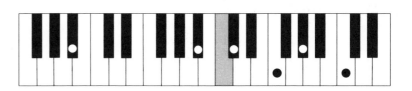

The B Collection

B major - B

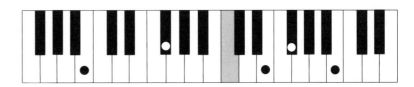

B suspended 4th - Bsus or Bsus4

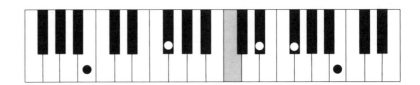

B augmented 5th - B+ or Baug

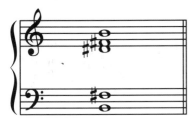

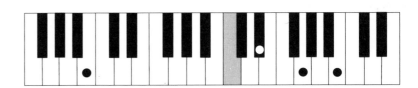

B added 6th - B6

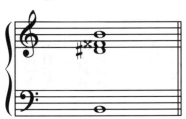

The B Collection

B

B major 7th - Bmaj7

B dominant 7th - B7

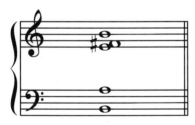

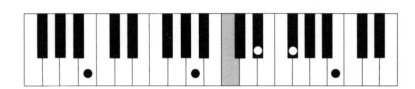

B dominant 7th with suspended 4th - B7sus or B7sus4

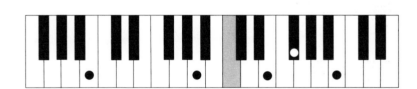

B dominant 7th with augmented 5th - B7+ or B7aug

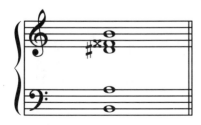

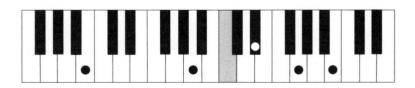

The B Collection

B dominant 7th with flattened 9th - B7(♭9)

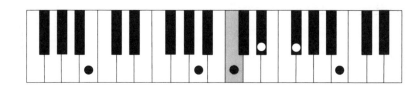

B added 9th - Badd9

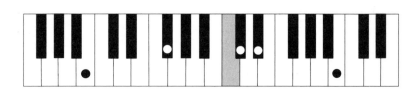

B major 9th - Bmaj9

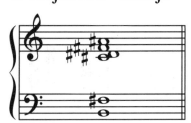

B dominant 9th - B9

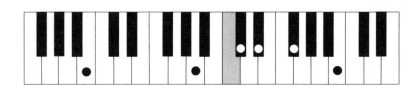

The B Collection

B dominant 9th with suspended 4th - B9sus or B9sus4

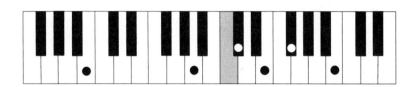

B dominant 9th with augmented 5th - B9+ or B9aug

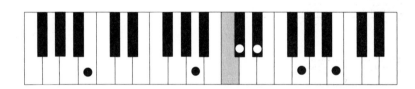

B dominant 11th - B11

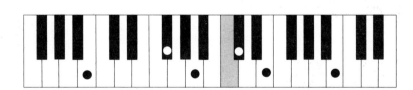

B dominant 11th with flattened 9th - B11(♭9)

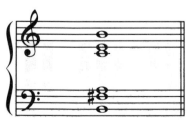
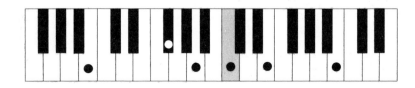

The B Collection

B dominant 13th - B13

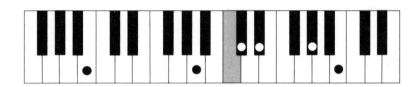

B minor - Bm

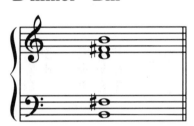

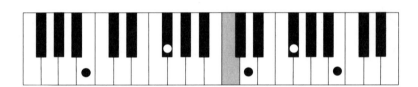

B diminished - B° or Bdim

B minor added 6th - Bm6

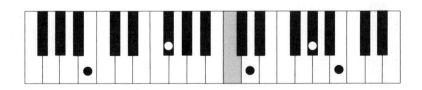

Your Own Collection

Why not use the charts below to notate your favourite chord voicings?

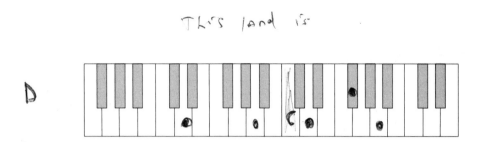

This land is

D

your land, This land is

G
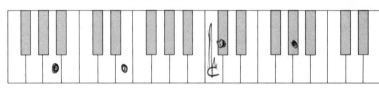

D — This land is my land

B — from Cali -

California To the New York

A7
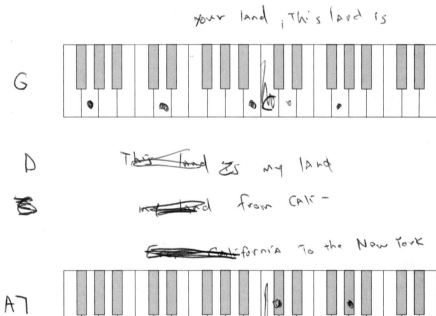

D — to the Harbor

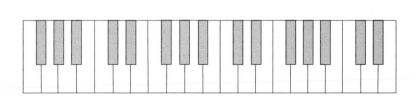

Your Own Collection

Why not use the charts below to notate your favourite chord voicings?

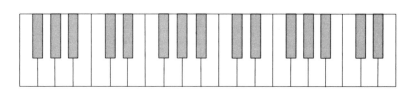

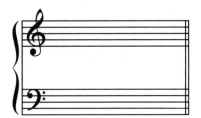

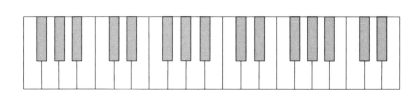

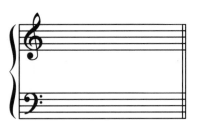

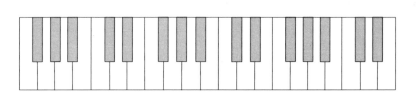

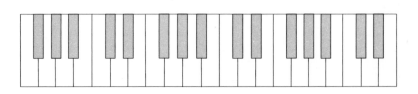

...and all that jazz! Great music for you to play from Music Sales